Fun With Shadows

By Sharon Siamon, Jeff Siamon and Cynthia Benjamin

Contents

Fun With Shadows

On a sunny day stand outside with the sun behind you. Look at the ground. It's your shadow! Wave your arms and your shadow's arms wave, too. Jump around and your shadow moves, too.

In this book you will discover how to make different shadow puppets with your hands and with sticks. You will learn how to use them, too. Then you can perform a shadow puppet show for your friends.

Hand Puppets

Shadow puppets are easy to make.
Your hands can be a shadow puppet.
You can use your hands to make many different shadows.

How to Make Hand Puppets

What You Need

- a wall in a dark room
- a torch
- a pair of hands

1. Shine the torch on the wall. It should be about 2 metres from the wall.
2. Choose an animal to make. Hold your hands in front of the wall. Follow the steps to make the animal.

Make a Spider

1. Cross one hand over the other to make the spider's legs.
2. Wiggle your fingers to move the legs.

Make a Dog

1. Bend your first finger to make the dog's eye. Point your thumb up to make the dog's ear.
2. Move your little finger up and down to make the dog bark.

Make a Swan

1. Bend one arm. Hold your other hand across the bend to make the swan's feathers.
2. Bend your first finger to make the swan's eye.
3. Use your thumb and fingers to make the swan open and shut its beak.

Where Does the Shadow Come From?

A shadow forms when an object blocks light. When you put your hands in front of the torch, your hands block some of the light. The light can't move through your hands, so a shadow appears on the wall.

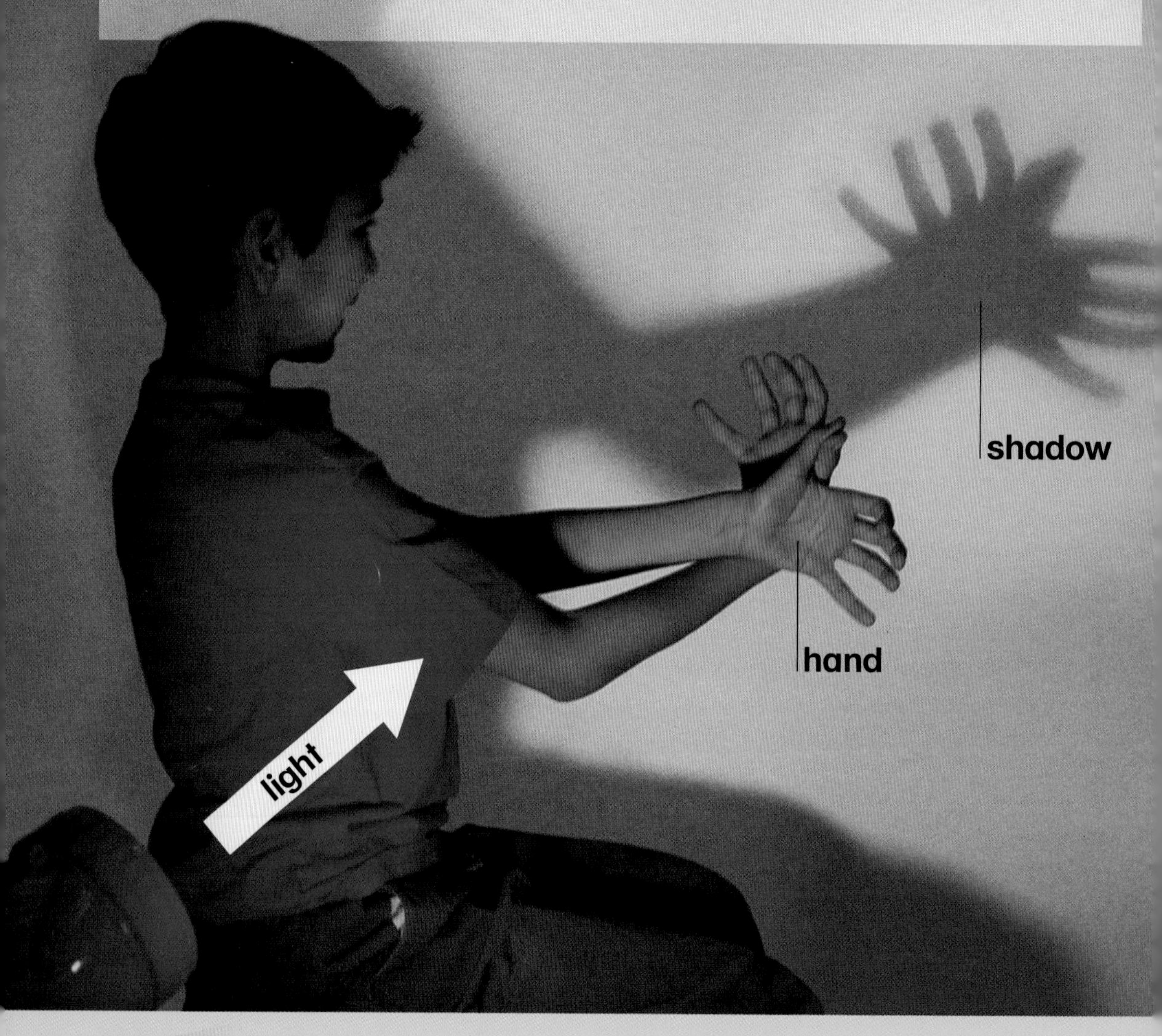

Try It!

You can make many other shadows with your hands. Can you work out how to make the shadows below? See how many other hand puppets you can make!

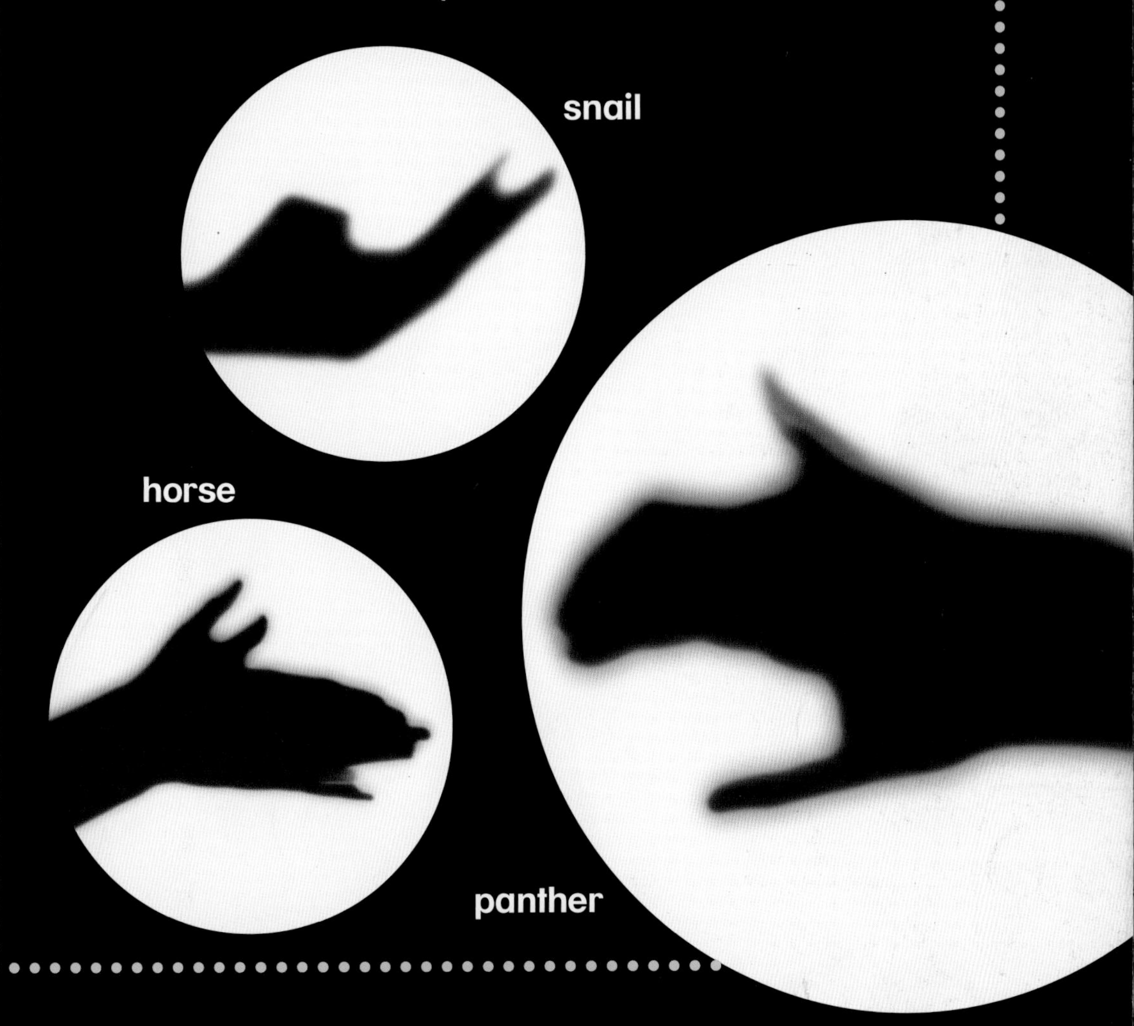

Stick Puppets

Shadow puppets have helped people tell stories for many years. Today people still use shadow puppets to tell stories.

Many shadow puppets have sticks attached to them. A puppeteer holds the stick to move the puppet and its shadow.

How to Make a Stick Puppet

What You Need

- card
- a pen or pencil
- scissors
- a thin stick
- tape
- a wall in a dark room
- a torch

1 Draw a shape on the card. It can be anything you like.

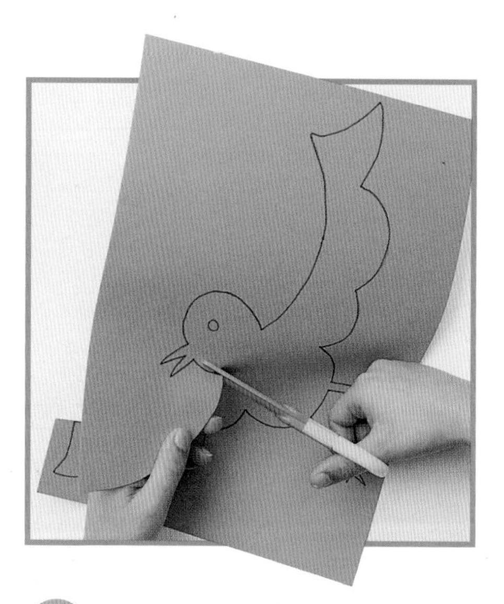

2 Cut out the shape.

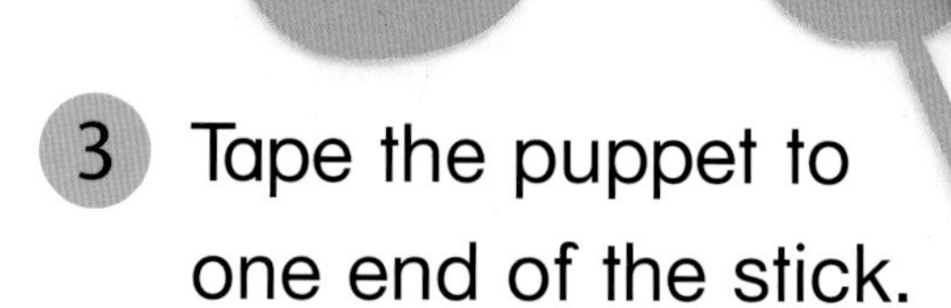

3 Tape the puppet to one end of the stick.

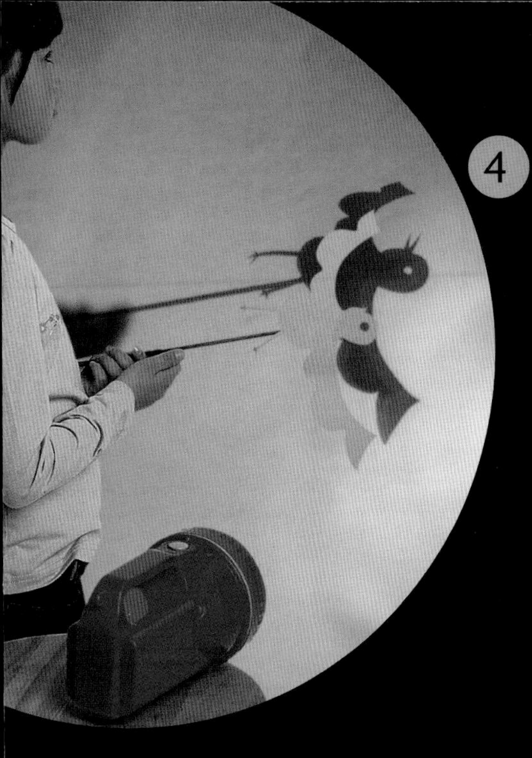

4 Shine the torch on the wall. Hold the puppet between the torch and the wall.

5 Move the puppet towards the torch to make the shadow bigger. Move it away from the torch to make the shadow smaller.

Why Does the Shadow Change Size?

When the puppet moves towards the torch, its shadow gets larger. That's because the puppet blocks more light. When the puppet moves away from the torch, its shadow gets smaller. That's because the puppet blocks less light.

Try It!

Try moving the torch instead of the puppet. What happens when you move the torch towards the puppet? What happens when you move it away from the puppet?

Put on a Show

You can use your hand and stick puppets to put on a shadow puppet show. Here are some tips.

- Use your puppets to tell a story.
- Ask a friend to perform with you. That way you can include more puppets in the show.
- Perform the show in a dark room. It will be easier to see the shadows on the wall.
- Have fun.